# Birds in Toyland

Appliqué a Whimsical Christmas Quilt from Piece O' Cake Designs

Becky Goldsmith *with* Linda Jenkins

C&T PUBLISHING

Text, photography, and artwork copyright © 2022 by Becky Goldsmith

Photography copyright © 2022 C&T Publishing, Inc.

Publisher: Amy Barrett-Daffin

Creative Director: Gailen Runge

Acquisitions Editor: Roxane Cerda

Managing/Developmental Editor: Liz Aneloski

Technical Editor: Debbie Rodgers

Cover/Book Designer: April Mostek

Production Coordinator: Tim Manibusan

Production Editors: Alice Mace Nakanishi and Jennifer Warren

Illustrators: Becky Goldsmith and Linda Johnson

Photography Coordinator: Lauren Herberg

Photography Assistant: Gabriel Martinez

Front cover photography by Becky Goldsmith

Instructional and "light quilt" photography by Becky Goldsmith; "dark quilt" and gallery photography by Lauren Herberg of C&T Publishing, Inc., unless otherwise noted

Published by C&T Publishing, Inc., P.O. Box 1456, Lafayette, CA 94549

Library of Congress Cataloging-in-Publication Data

Names: Goldsmith, Becky, 1956- author. | Jenkins, Linda, 1943- author. | Piece O' Cake Designs.

Title: Birds in toyland : appliqué a whimsical Christmas quilt from Piece O' Cake designs / Becky Goldsmith, Linda Jenkins.

Description: Lafayette : C&T Publishing, 2022.

Identifiers: LCCN 2021053370 | ISBN 9781644031599 (trade paperback) | ISBN 9781644031605 (ebook)

Subjects: LCSH: Appliqué--Patterns. | Quilting--Patterns. | Christmas decorations. | Birds in art.

Classification: LCC TT779 .G629445 2022 | DDC 746.44/5041--dc23/eng/20211103

LC record available at https://lccn.loc.gov/2021053370

Printed in the USA

10 9 8 7 6 5 4 3 2 1

## A Word from the Author

Linda, my friend and retired business partner, wanted to make a new holiday quilt featuring festive birds. Linda's ideas are good, so I got to work and darned if she wasn't right. The birds in this quilt are more than just cute, they have personality. 🙂

I am still, and always will be, grateful to Linda for her friendship, support, and her excellent ideas!

Special thanks go to my friend, Polly Clarke Stephenson, who came up with the name "Birds in Toyland." Thank you, Polly! I value your friendship, even though we don't see each other often enough.

# Contents

# Introduction

*Birds in Toyland* is a very happy quilt. You will find yourself smiling as you stitch, which is a wonderful thing.

The blocks are very versatile:

- You can make the quilt with pieced blocks, as shown, or you can set the blocks with simple sashing.

- You can use individual blocks to make smaller quilts, pillows, and/or totes.

- You can enlarge or reduce the block patterns.

- You can use the blocks in other quilts!

There are so many options that I can't think of them all—but you can! ☺

## You Are the Boss of the Birds!

Before you begin, you need to make some key decisions about your *Birds in Toyland* quilt. Your answers to these questions will help you to choose the correct fabrics, supplies, and will lead you to the pertinent instructions for each technique.

- **Will your quilt have light or dark backgrounds?** Once you decide, use *either* the Cutting for the Quilt with LIGHT Backgrounds (page 13) or Cutting for the Quilt with DARK Backgrounds (page 15), not both.

- **You get to choose what size your appliqué blocks will be!** Follow the instructions on each pattern page to print them full size at either 8″ × 8″ or 10″ × 10″ (see Appliqué Patterns, page 65). There are some tiny appliqué shapes and some of you will prefer the larger size.

  Once you decide which size blocks you want to make, be sure to follow the yardage and cutting instructions for that size. Yardage and instructions for 8″ × 8″ blocks are listed first, 10″ × 10″ blocks are in parentheses.

- **Are you appliquéing with felted wool, cotton, or both wool and cotton?** There are detailed how-to instructions for both felted wool (see Wool Appliqué Techniques, page 29) and needle-turn hand appliqué with cotton (see Cotton Appliqué Techniques, page 22).

- **Are you keen to add some bling to your quilt?** You will see how easy it is to add sequins and beads to your quilt to make it even more festive (see Embellishments, page 36).

**Birds in Toyland** by Becky Goldsmith

Wool with light backgrounds

**Birds in Toyland III by Linda Jenkins**

Wool appliqué and cotton pieced blocks with dark backgrounds

# Fabric and Notions

## Choosing Fabrics

Choose a variety of fabrics from your stash, go shopping, or both! Choose colors that make you smile. You will be handling them a lot, so the more you love them, the happier you will be.

Choose your background fabric(s) first. Whether light or dark, neutral or a color, your background will influence all the other colors you choose to use in your quilt.

### FINISHED SIZES

**Blocks:** 8″ × 8″ (or 10″ × 10″)

**Quilt:** 48″ × 48″ with 8″ blocks (or 60″ × 60″ with 10″ blocks)

### FABRIC

*Yardage is based on 40″ of usable width of fabric.*

> **note**
> The first number in the lists at right is for 8″ blocks and the second number (in parentheses) is for 10″ blocks.

*Use LIGHT background fabric to make a LIGHT quilt or DARK background fabric to make a DARK quilt.*

- **Appliqué block backgrounds:** 1 or more fabrics to equal 1⅞ yards (2⅞ yards)
- **Pieced block backgrounds:** 1⅓ yards (1¾ yards)

**Pieced block accent fabric (dark or light):** ⅔ yard (⅞ yard)

**Appliqué:** A variety of fat quarters, large scraps of felted wool, and/or woven cloth

**Straight binding:** ½ yard (⅝ yard)

**Backing and sleeve:** 3⅜ yards (4 yards)

**Batting:** 56″ × 56″ (68″ × 68″)

# NOTIONS

**Self-laminating sheets:** 9″ × 12″ clear, single-sided, heavyweight; 18 sheets (20 sheets) for templates

**Black ultrafine-tip permanent marker:** For writing on the vinyl. I like the Sharpie Ultra Fine Point Permanent Marker; other markers may not work on vinyl.

**12-gauge vinyl:** 2 (3) rolls of 16″ × 1½ yards to make overlay (I use Premium Clear Vinyl by C&T Publishing.)

**Paper-backed fusible web:** 2 packs of 10 sheets for wool appliqué (I use SoftFuse Premium by Shades Textiles.)

**Teflon pressing sheet:** To use with paper-backed fusible web

**Optional for wool appliqué:** *Temporary fabric glue stick*

**Small paper scissors**

**Small and medium fabric scissors**

**Invisible appliqué needles:** I use Clover's Black Gold #12 Appliqué Needle, Tulip's #11 Appliqué Needle, and/or Clover's Gold Eye #12 Appliqué Needle.

**Crewel needle:** Bohin's #9 Crewel Needle for wool appliqué and embroidery

**Appliqué pins:** I recommend Bohin's ½″ Appliqué/Sequin Pins, Karen Kay Buckley's Shorter Perfect Pins, Little House Appliqué Pins, and ¾″ Clover's Appliqué Pins.

**Fine, strong 100% cotton thread:** I recommend Super Bobs Cotton by Superior Threads. Prewound bobbins with 50-weight 2-ply MasterPiece thread.

**Wool thread:** For wool appliqué

**Perle cotton #12 thread or embroidery floss:** For embroidery

**White charcoal pencil:** For medium to dark fabrics (I use General's Charcoal White Pencil.)

**Firm graphite pencil:** For light fabrics (I use Blackwing 602 graphite pencil.)

**Pencil sharpener:** I recommend Blackwing Two-Step Long Point Sharpener.

**Optional pencils:** *Sewline Fabric Pencil or similar 9mm mechanical pencil in white and gray*

**Sandpaper board:** Or use a sheet of fine-grain sandpaper.

**Round wooden toothpicks**

**Sealable bags:** For your templates

**Embellishments:** Sequins, beads, buttons, ribbon, and trims to embellish your quilt

**Good light**

**Optional:** *Pillow or lap desk to rest your forearms on as you sew*

# General Instructions

## Using the Block Patterns

You have two options for using the block patterns.

### OPTION 1: *Enlarging the Blocks*

Make copies of the blocks (see Appliqué Patterns, page 65), enlarging them by the percentage noted on the patterns. You can do this in one step on a copier with 11″ × 14″ paper; or make a copy of the right and left halves of the block on 8½″ × 11″ paper, and then trim and tape them together.

### OPTION 2: *Downloading the Blocks*

You can download and print full-size patterns using the following link:

*tinyurl.com/11467-patterns-download*

## Making the Appliqué Templates and Placement Overlays

Make templates (see Hand Appliqué Templates, page 17) and placement overlays (see Make a Placement Overlay, page 17) from your full-size patterns.

## Fabric Preparation

- Cotton fabric shrinks, and you can't tell by look or feel how much an individual fabric might shrink.

- Fabric dyes can bleed when wet. Water chemistry, which varies from place to place, has an impact on dye migration.

- Fabric off-the-bolt has been treated with a wide array of chemicals that cause allergic reactions in some people.

I always wash my fabric in the washer and dry it in the dryer before using it, to remove excess dyes and chemicals, and to shrink it to its final size. I don't add any "spray" products to fabrics before I use them. I press with steam and sometimes a spritz of water. Washed fabric feels and smells nice and it has a nap that helps to hold shapes in place as you pin and sew.

When washing fabric or a finished quilt, use a neutral detergent without added softeners. Retro Wash Laundry Powder (by Retro Clean) or Orvus WA Paste (by Proctor & Gamble) are good choices. All Free Clear detergent (by Henkel Corporation) works. It does have softeners but is available at most grocery stores. Add Shout Color Catchers (by S. C. Johnson & Son, Inc.), Retayne (by G&K Craft Industries), and/or Synthrapol (by Jacquard) to the wash to deal with dye migration. I wash in hot water, rinse in cool.

> *note*
>
> Felted wool does not need to be washed before using, unless you know you will be washing the finished quilt. If you do wash felted wool, be gentle with it, so it doesn't shrink more.
>
> Carefully wash or dry clean quilts made with felted wool. Be aware that colors may run.

## Audition Your Fabrics

Every individual piece of fabric has an impact on your quilt. Use a design wall and "audition" each piece as you go, so you can see how the blocks and borders look before you sew anything together. The audition process takes time, but once the blocks are sewn, you won't want to unsew to make changes.

For ideas and inspiration, refer to the photos shown in Appliqué Blocks (page 40).

## Seam Allowances

A $3/16''$ seam allowance—also known as a scant $1/4''$—is perfect for needle-turn hand appliqué. Less than that can cause the raw edges to fray; more can cause the seam allowance to bunch up.

Felted wool appliqué shapes do not require a seam allowance.

Use a $1/4''$ seam allowance for machine piecing.

# Cutting the Backgrounds, Accent Pieces, and Binding, and Construction for the Pieced Setting Blocks

## Cutting for the Quilt with LIGHT Backgrounds

*WOF = width of fabric*

> **note** ···················································································
> The first number in the lists at right is for 8″ blocks and the
> second number (in parentheses) is for 10″ blocks.

### CUTTING LIGHT BACKGROUNDS, DARK ACCENT PIECES, AND BINDING

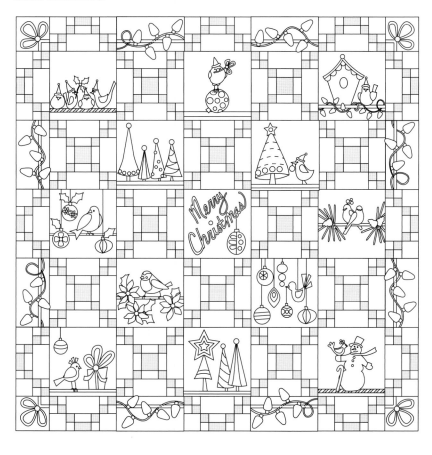

### Light backgrounds for appliqué blocks

- Cut 5 strips 10″ × WOF. (Cut 7 strips 12″ × WOF.)

  Subcut 13 squares 10″ × 10″ (12″ × 12″).

  Subcut 8 rectangles 6″ × 10″ (7″ × 12″).

- Cut 1 strip 6″ × WOF.
  (Cut 1 strip 7″ × WOF.)

  Subcut 4 squares 6″ × 6″ (7″ × 7″).

### Light backgrounds for pieced blocks

- Cut 12 strips 2½″ × WOF.
  (Cut 13 strips 3″ × WOF.)
  Set aside 2 strips for Step 5.

  Subcut 60 rectangles 2½″ × 4½″.
  (Subcut 60 rectangles 3″ × 5½″).

  Subcut 24 squares 2½″ × 2½″.
  (Subcut 24 squares 3″ × 3″).

- Cut 10 strips 1½″ × WOF.
  (Cut 11 strips 1¾″ × WOF.)

### Dark accent for pieced blocks

- Cut 2 strips 2½″ × WOF.
  (Cut 2 strips 3″ × WOF.)

- Cut 10 strips 1½″ × WOF.
  (Cut 11 strips 1¾″ × WOF.)

- Cut fabric for appliqué as needed.

### Binding

- Cut 6 (7) strips 2½″ × WOF for double-fold binding.

# Piecing the LIGHT Background Setting Blocks

**1.** Sew 1 light background 1½″ (1¾″) × WOF strip to one dark accent 1½″ (1¾″) × WOF strip. Press the seam allowances to the dark strip. Repeat to make 6 (7).

**2.** Subcut 144 units 1½″ (1¾″) wide.

**3.** Sew the units together to make 72 four-patches.

**4.** Sew 1 light background 1½″ (1¾″) × WOF strip to each side of a dark accent 2½″ (3″) × WOF strip. Press the seam allowances to the dark strip. Repeat to make 2.

Subcut 12 A units 1½″ (1¾″) wide.

Subcut 12 B units 2½″ (3″) wide.

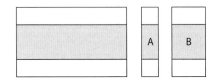

**5.** Sew 1 dark accent 1½″ (1¾″) × WOF strip to each side of a light background 2½″ (3″) × WOF strip. Press the seam allowances to the dark strip. Repeat to make 2.

**6.** Subcut 36 C units 1½″ (1¾″) wide.

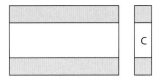

**7.** Sew together an A and C unit. Press to the C unit. Make 12.

**8.** Sew a C unit to each side of a B unit. Press to the C units. Make 12.

**9.** Assemble the light background rectangles and pieced units to make 1 pieced block. Sew the strips and units together in rows, press to the background rectangles.

**10.** Sew the rows together to make 1 block, pressing to the center. Repeat to make 12 pieced blocks.

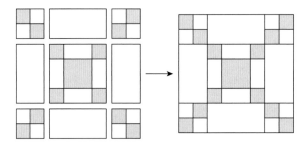

**11.** Assemble the light background squares and rectangles, and pieced units to make 1 pieced border block. Sew the squares or rectangles and units together in rows, press to the background pieces.

**12.** Sew the rows together to make 1 border block, pressing to the center. Repeat to make 12 pieced border blocks.

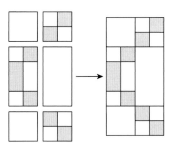

# Cutting for the Quilt with DARK Backgrounds

*WOF = width of fabric*

> **note** ............................................
> The first number in the lists below and at right is for 8″ blocks and the second number (in parentheses) is for 10″ blocks.

## Dark backgrounds for pieced blocks

- Cut 12 strips 2½″ × WOF. (Cut 13 strips 3″ × WOF.) Set aside 2 strips for Step 5.

  Subcut 60 rectangles 2½″ × 4½″. (Subcut 60 rectangles 3″ × 5½″).

  Subcut 24 squares 2½″ × 2½″. (Subcut 24 squares 3″ × 3″).

- Cut 10 strips 1½″ × WOF. (Cut 11 strips 1¾″ × WOF.)

## Light accent for pieced blocks

- Cut 2 strips 2½″ × WOF. (Cut 12 strips 3″ × WOF.)

- Cut 10 strips 1½″ × WOF. (Cut 11 strips 1¾″ × WOF.)

- Cut the fabric for the appliqués as needed.

## Binding

- Cut 6 (7) strips 2½″ × WOF for double-fold binding.

## CUTTING DARK BACKGROUNDS, LIGHT ACCENT PIECES, AND BINDING

### Dark backgrounds for appliqué blocks

- Cut 5 strips 10″ × WOF. (Cut 7 strips 12″ × WOF.)

  Subcut 13 squares 10″ × 10″ (12″ × 12″).

  Subcut 8 rectangles 6″ × 10″ (7″ × 12″).

- Cut 1 strip 6″ × WOF. (Cut 1 strip 7″ × WOF.)

  Subcut 4 squares 6″ × 6″ (7″ × 7″).

# Piecing the DARK Background Setting Blocks

**1.** Sew 1 dark background 1½″ (1¾″) × WOF strip to one light accent 1½″ (1¾″) × WOF strip. Press the seam allowances to the dark strip. Repeat to make 6 (7).

**2.** Subcut 144 units 1½″ (1¾″) wide.

**3.** Sew the units together to make 72 four-patches.

**4.** Sew 1 dark background 1½″ (1¾″) × WOF strip to each side of a light accent 2½″ (3″) × WOF strip. Press the seam allowances to the dark strips. Repeat to make 2.

Subcut 12 A units 1½″ (1¾″) wide.

Subcut 12 B units 2½″ (3″) wide.

**5.** Sew 1 light accent 1½″ (1¾″) × WOF strip to each side of a dark background 2½″ (3″) × WOF strip. Press the seam allowances to the dark strip. Repeat to make 2.

**6.** Subcut 36 C units 1½″ (1¾″) wide.

**7.** Sew together an A and C unit. Press to the C unit. Make 12.

**8.** Sew a C unit to each side of a B unit. Press to the C units. Make 12.

**9.** Assemble the dark background rectangles and pieced units to make 1 pieced block. Sew the rectangles and units together in rows, press to the background rectangles.

**10.** Sew the rows together to make 1 block, pressing to the center. Repeat to make 12 pieced blocks.

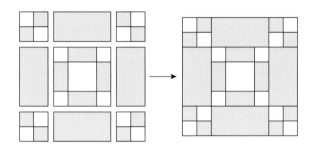

**11.** Assemble the dark background squares, rectangles, and pieced units to make 1 pieced border block. Sew the squares or rectangles and units together in rows, press to the dark background pieces.

**12.** Sew the rows together to make 1 border block, pressing to the center. Repeat to make 12 pieced border blocks.

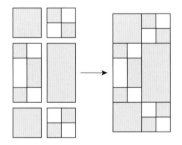

# Appliqué Instructions

## Hand Appliqué Templates

In needle-turn appliqué, templates are the finished size—no seam allowances are added. Use the templates right side up on the right side of the fabric. Keep the shapes for each block together.

Use single-sided laminate sheets, available at an office supply store. If you would like your templates to have more substance, copy the shapes onto white card stock. (English Paper-Piecing Specialty Paper from C&T Publishing is a good choice.)

**1.** Make 2–3 copies of each block and border pattern (see Appliqué Patterns, page 65) onto plain paper or card stock. Each shape requires its own template. You will need more than one copy for areas where shapes overlap.

**2.** Trim away the excess paper, leaving a "buffer" approximately ¼˝ wide around the shapes.

**3.** Place a self-adhesive laminating sheet, shiny side down, on the table. Peel off the paper backing, leaving the sticky side of the sheet faceup.

**4.** Hold the paper copy with the drawn side down. *Cup* it (with the center lower than the sides you are holding) and smoothly lower it onto the sticky side of the self-laminating sheet.

**5.** Cut out each shape, splitting the drawn line with your scissors. Do not cut outside of the lines, as it adds to the size of the template. Keep the edges smooth and the points sharp.

## Make a Placement Overlay

The placement overlay allows you to accurately position your shapes on the block without tracing on your background fabric and eliminates the need to use a lightbox.

**1.** Make 1 copy of each block and border pattern (see Appliqué Patterns, page 65).

**2.** Cut a piece of clear 12-gauge vinyl to the finished size of each block.

**3.** Tape the pattern onto a table to keep it from shifting out of place. Tape the vinyl over the pattern.

**4.** Use a black ultrafine-tip Sharpie marker to draw the horizontal and vertical center lines onto the vinyl.

Draw an X in the upper right-hand corner of the overlay.

**5.** Trace the pattern and the numbers onto the vinyl. If your pen goes off the line, just pick it up and move it back in place. You won't be graded on how well you trace. 😊

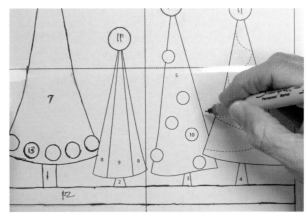

## Prepare the Background Blocks

**1.** Press the block and border backgrounds in half, horizontally and vertically. The pressed-in grid aligns with the drawn grid on the placement overlay.

**2.** Draw a short line on each end of the pressed-in lines at the raw edges of the fabric. These short lines help when you position the placement overlay on the block.

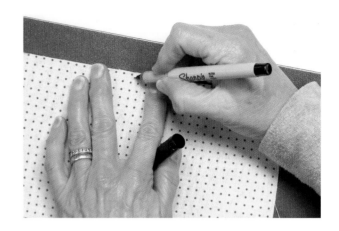

## Prepare the Needle-Turn Appliqué Shapes

*If the appliqué piece is narrow and/or small, see Cutaway Appliqué (page 27) as an option.*

**1.** Place your appliqué fabric right side up on a sandpaper board. The sandpaper keeps the fabric from shifting as you trace.

**2.** Place the template right side up on the fabric, with as many edges on the bias as possible, or place the template on the fabric to take advantage of a design in the fabric.

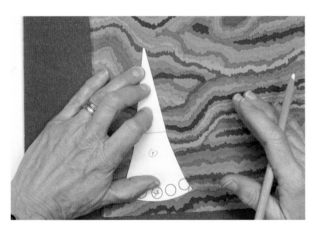

> ### note
> A bias edge turns under more gracefully than an edge on the straight of grain. Ignore the grain line if there is a design in the fabric that you want to capture.

**3.** Trace around the template. Make a line you can see! This line will be turned to the back of the shape as you sew.

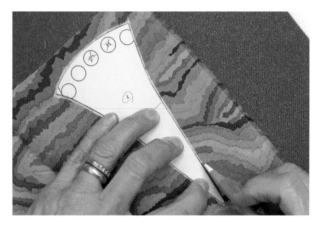

**4.** Cut away the excess fabric leaving a ³⁄₁₆″ seam allowance. Leave a slightly larger seam allowance on edges that lie underneath another appliqué shape.

## Audition Your Appliqué Blocks

The only way to know how your colors look together is if you can see them in place, cut to size and shape, on the design wall. The audition process is important. I often design the entire quilt before I begin appliquéing the blocks.

For ideas and inspiration, refer to the photos shown in Appliqué Blocks (page 40).

**1.** Place the appliqué block backgrounds on your design wall. If you are using different fabrics, play with the placement until they feel right to you.

**2.** Work on one block at a time and trace the appliqué shapes and cut them out, adding a ³⁄₁₆″ seam allowance on needle-turn shapes.

**3.** Whether you are working with cotton or wool fabrics, take time to evaluate your color choices as your block takes shape on the wall. Now is the time to play! If you get stuck trying to find the perfect color/fabric for any shape, move on and come back to it later.

**4.** Trust your choices. This is your quilt—you will know when your block is ready to sew.

## Needle and Thread Choices for Appliqué with Cotton

### Needle Choices

"Sharps" needles are medium length and commonly used for hand appliqué. They have a sharp point to pierce the fabric cleanly. Longer milliners/straw needles are also used for hand appliqué. Use the smallest needle, in the style you prefer, that is comfortable in your hand. In hand-sewing needles, the higher number, the smaller the needle.

### Thread Choices

Thread color and thickness have a lot to do with how invisible your stitches are. Choose a fine 50–80-weight 2-ply thread in the color that most closely matches your appliqué fabric.

I use Superior Threads' 50-weight 2-ply cotton thread (only on prewound bobbins) for most of my hand appliqué.

## Needle and Thread Choices for Appliqué with Wool

If you want the stitches to be less visible, use a wool thread that is a close match to the appliqué fabric in both color and value.

If you want the stitches to show, use thicker thread in the same or contrasting color. Perle cotton comes in a variety of weights and colors and is a good choice for showy stitches. Flower thread is unmercerized 12-weight perle cotton with a matte finish that blends nicely into felted wool.

Match your needle to your thread. Embroidery needles come in a variety of sizes and work well. I like the crewel #9 needle made by Bohin.

# Appliqué the Blocks

*There are a few light bulbs in the border blocks that extend over the block seamline and will need to be appliquéd after the blocks are sewn together.*

**1.** Place the background right side up on top of a sandpaper board. The sandpaper keeps the background from shifting as you position appliqué pieces on the block. If you don't have a sandpaper board, try working on top of a rotary cutting mat.

**2.** Position the placement overlay right side up on top of the background, matching the center lines on the overlay with the pressed-in grid in the fabric.

**3.** Before placing appliqué pieces on the block, finger-press the seam allowance to the back of the appliqué shape. **Do not skip this step.** You'll be amazed at how much easier this one step makes needle-turning the turn-under allowance.

> *tip* **Finger-Press** ········································
>
> Turn the seam allowance to the back of the shape, making sure the drawn line is pressed to the back. Use your fingertips to press a crease along the inside edge of the drawn line anywhere it will be turned under and sewn.

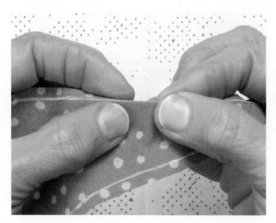

**4.** Place the appliqué pieces under the overlay, on top of the background, using the drawn lines for guidance. Do not turn the seam allowances under at this time.

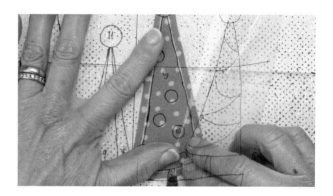

**5.** Remove the vinyl overlay before pinning and stitching.

## Pin the Appliqué in Place

I recommend short/fine pins with small heads because they stay out of your way as you sew.

**1.** Pin with the block flat on your board to prevent shapes from shifting out of position.

**2.** Position the pins parallel to and ¼˝ inside of the drawn line.

**3.** Pick up a pin and push the point of it through both layers of fabric. You will feel the sandpaper board below.

**4.** Place the index finger of your other hand about ¼˝ away from the point of the pin and push the fabric down toward the sandpaper board.

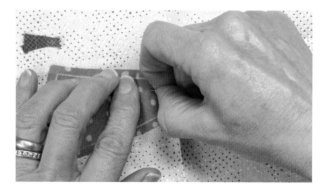

**5.** With your index finger still in place on the fabric, lift the pin up just enough, so you can slide the pin forward underneath the background fabric. It is okay if the pin scrapes the sandpaper.

**6.** Continue pinning in this manner until the appliqué shape is held neatly to the block. If you think the shape may have moved during pinning, check it with the placement overlay.

## Pin the Outer Points

Outer points are pinned differently than the rest of the appliqué to keep the points in position as you sew.

**1.** Identify the side of the point you will sew first, as you approach the point. For right-handers sewing from right to left, this will be the side to the right of the point. (It's the opposite for left-handers.)

**2.** Place your pin parallel to and ¼″ from the side of the outer point you will sew first, on top of the line that marks the second side of the point.

**3.** This pin can be removed when the first side of the point has been sewn in place.

## Off-the-Block Construction

When one appliqué shape lies on top of another, and they share the same outer edge, sew them together "off-the-block." This will make turning the seam allowances at their shared edge easier.

**1.** Leave extra fabric around the bottom shape to make it easier to hold.

**2.** Finger-press, position, and pin the top shape in place.

**3.** Appliqué the top shape to the bottom shape.

**4.** Trim away the excess fabric from the combined shapes.

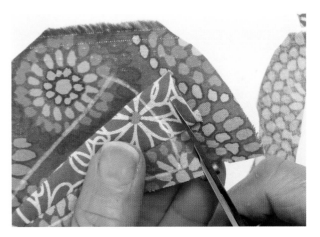

**5.** Finger-press and appliqué the unit to the block, turning under both seam allowances together at the shared edge.

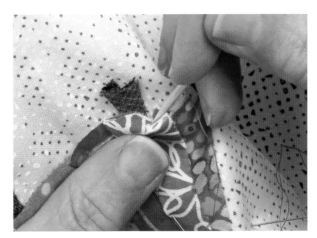

# Cotton Appliqué Techniques

## Make an Invisible Appliqué Stitch

In needle-turn appliqué, you usually use the needle to turn under the seam allowance, but there are times when a round wooden toothpick or your fingertips work better than the needle. Use what works best at any given time.

When you are sewing nearly straight edges, you can turn under enough seam allowance to make several stitches. In other places you will only be able to turn under one stitch at a time in order to keep the edge smooth. The pace of your stitching changes as the shape changes.

The most common stitch direction is from right to left. Left-handers typically mirror this stitch.

**1.** Hold the block, so the edge to stitch is roughly level with the horizon. Work over the top edge of the appliqué, with the seam allowance away from you.

**2.** Bring your thread up through the finger-pressed fold in the appliqué, just inside the chalk line. This ensures that the knot and tail of the thread will be hidden between the appliqué and the background.

**3.** Position the needle, so it goes straight down into the background fabric, next to the appliqué, right next to the place where the thread came out of the appliqué fabric.

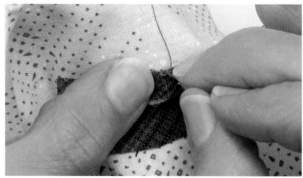

Imagine that the needle is a diver cleanly entering the water. The needle "dives" into the background fabric, next to the edge of the appliqué. Like a diver enters the water at a 90° angle, so should your needle go through the fabric with each stitch.

**4.** Rock the needle over the tip of your middle or index finger underneath the block and push the needle forward, under the background, following the edge of the appliqué.

**5.** Turn the needle point up and push the needle through the fabric, just catching the folded edge of the appliqué. Do not let the needle travel diagonally through the layers as this causes stitches that can "gather up" when the thread is pulled tight.

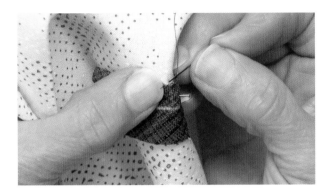

**6.** The position of the hand holding the fabric is important. Place your thumb on top of the folded edge of the appliqué about a stitch-length away from the beginning of the stitch, so the needle is pointed at the end (not the side) of your thumb as you take a stitch.

As you rock off your bottom fingertip, the thumb holds the layers of fabric together, so your stitch will go straight up through the fabric, rather than on the diagonal.

## Appliqué Outer Points

Outer points are tricky because of the amount of seam allowance that falls beneath the point. Once you know how to deal with that, sewing the point is a "piece o' cake"!

**1.** Finger-press an outer point, making sure to press the drawn line under, beyond the end of the point, on both sides of the point. You will have 2 crossed finger-pressed lines at the point.

**2.** Use the placement overlay to position the appliqué shape on the block (see Appliqué the Blocks, page 20). Pin it in place (see Pin the Outer Points, page 21).

**3.** Sew toward the outer point. When you are $3/16''$ away from the point, begin taking shorter/closer stitches.

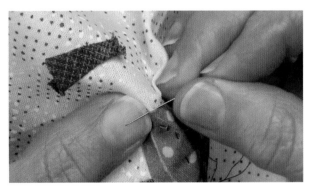

**4.** Sew to the point and take a stitch in place (a tack stitch) before you begin turning under the seam allowance at the point.

**5.** Remove the pin at the point. Turn the block in your hand, so you are in position to sew the second side of the point. Place the toothpick over the fold in the turn-under allowance with the tip of the toothpick even with the cut edge of the seam allowance.

**6.** Imagine the way a windshield wiper moves, as you push against fabric with the toothpick and rotate the seam allowance underneath the point. Let the toothpick pivot on top of the point as the tip end moves the fabric under the point.

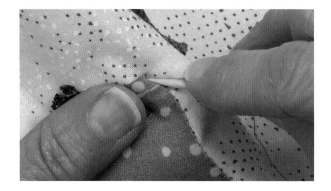

**7.** Gently pull the thread out from the point to elongate the point. Reach under the point with the toothpick and use it to sweep the seam allowance away from the point, so it lies smooth. Never scoop the turn-under allowance back toward the point—there is no room for any more fabric at the point.

**8.** If you need to turn under more seam allowance, place the dampened toothpick next to the fold. "Windshield-wiper" the fabric under, again letting the toothpick pivot at the tack stitch.

**9.** Continue in this manner, rotating fabric under the point and then sweeping it away from the point, until the chalk line is turned under and the seam allowance feels smooth under the point.

**10.** Use shorter/closer stitches until you are past the bulkiness at the point.

# Appliqué Inner Points

Slow down, give inner points your full attention, and you will be happy with the results.

**1.** Finger-press beyond the end of the chalk lines into the body of the appliqué piece at each inner point. The finger-pressed creases should cross each other.

**2.** Use the placement overlay to position the appliqué piece on the block. Pin it in place.

**3.** Sew toward the inner point. When you can no longer turn the turn-under allowance without distorting it, you must clip the inner point.

**4.** The clip needs to be perfectly centered. Clip to and just barely through the chalk line. The end of the clip should be at the inside edge of the finger-pressed crease. To cut accurately, center the inner cutting side of the top blade to where you need to cut.

**5.** Use a dampened toothpick to gently turn under the seam allowance on the first side of the inner point. Do not poke, scoop, twirl, or pull the seam allowance. Use the side of the toothpick to gently pat it under on the finger-pressed fold.

**6.** When you are within ³⁄₁₆″ of the point, begin making the stitches closer together and farther into the appliqué. Take your cue from the fabric. The key to a successful inner point is not to let the fabric fray.

*tip* **But My Stitches Will Show!** ·················
You have to catch more of the appliqué fabric at an inner point because if you don't, your fabric will fray. Yes, your stitches will show—but they will show less if:

• Your thread color is a good match to the fabric

• Stitches get bigger (and then smaller) gradually, but are not so close as to resemble a satin stitch.

• Stitches are perpendicular to the edge of the appliqué

Stitches at the inner point should look like this:

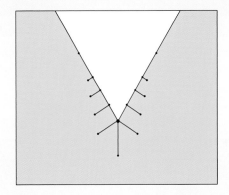

**7.** I like to take a tack stitch at the deepest part of the inner point. The needle goes into the background at the deepest part of the V and comes out exactly where the thread is coming out of the appliqué.

**8.** Work the second side of the inner point in the same manner. Make the stitches so they gradually move closer to the edge of the appliqué until you have a seam allowance again.

## Appliqué Outer Curves and Circles

The seam allowance on outer curves can pleat and make points on what should be a smooth outer edge. If you deal with these pleats as they form, they will no longer be a problem.

**1.** Cut an accurate ³⁄₁₆″ seam allowance, especially on circles. Too big and the fabric pleats easily, too small and the fabric frays, making it harder to turn.

**2.** Finger-press outer curves and circles with a series of short, overlapping lines that follow the curve.

**3.** Use the point of the needle to grab the middle of the seam allowance and turn under enough to make one stitch. Sometimes you can avoid pleats entirely by turning under only enough for one stitch.

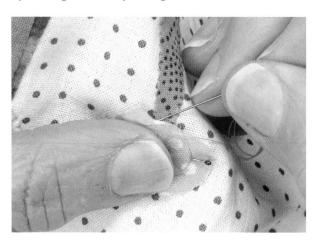

**4.** When pleats do form, take the time to fan them open. Reach into the fold of the pleat with either a toothpick or your needle. Sweep the fabric in the pleat to the right. Take out the toothpick and reinsert it behind the pleat and sweep the fabric in the pleat to the left.

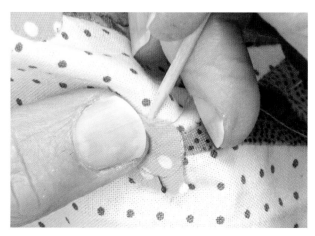

**5.** Once you smooth out the pleat, continue stitching in this manner. When another pleat forms, repeat the process. Outer curves are very pretty if you take the time to do them well.

## Appliqué Inner Curves

**1.** To ensure a smooth inner curve, cut a minimum of 3 clips on any curve. If the curve is long, you will need to make more clips. Make your first clip at the deepest/center of the inner curve.

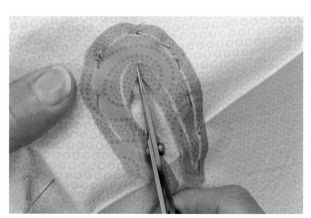

**2.** Clip at a 90° angle to the chalk line. Move your scissors with every cut and clip at a 90° angle to the chalk line. In most cases the clip should stop just shy of the finger-pressed fold.

*tip* **Clipping Tip** ·············································
Tightly woven fabrics will require clips that are deeper and closer together. Loosely woven fabrics will stretch at the end of the clip, so clips can be a little farther apart and less deep.

**3.** Sweep the length of the clipped seam allowance under with the side of your toothpick, toward your holding thumb.

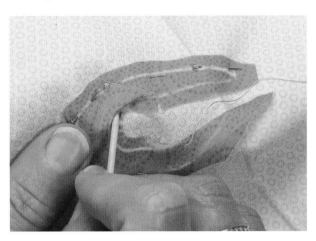

**4.** Clipped seam allowances can fray. Make your stitches a little closer together and catch a little more of the appliqué fabric than normal through the clipped area.

## Cutaway Appliqué

Use cutaway appliqué on narrow and/or small shapes such as the letters in "Merry Christmas," the Christmas light cords, hat trim, and bird beaks.

If the appliqué piece that you audition has been cut to size, you will need to prepare a new shape with extra fabric around it.

**1.** Place the appliqué fabric right side up on your sandpaper board. Place the template on it, leaving ½"–¾" of fabric around the template. Trace around the template.

**2.** Cut out the appliqué piece, leaving ½"–¾" of excess fabric around the traced shape.

**3.** Finger-press the seam allowances to the back of the fabric along the inside edge of the drawn line. Don't worry about the excess fabric; it will be cut off as you sew.

**4.** Use the placement overlay to position the appliqué piece on the block.

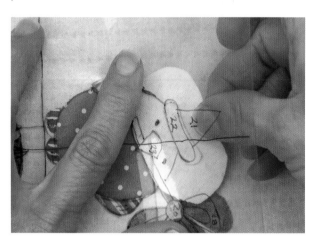

**5.** Pin it in place. Place pins parallel to and ¼″ away from the side of the shape that you will sew first. Remove the pins as you sew the opposite side of the shape.

**6.** Begin cutting away the excess fabric leaving a ³⁄₁₆″ turn-under allowance. On very small shapes, use a scant ³⁄₁₆″ seam allowance.

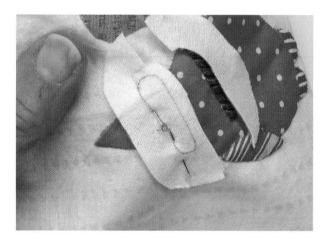

**7.** Turn the seam allowance under and begin stitching. Trim away more seam allowance, as necessary.

# Wool Appliqué Techniques

## Felted Wool or Wool Felt?

Felted wool and wool felt are two very different kinds of cloth and both can be used in wool appliqué. Neither has a right or wrong side—choose the side you like best.

Wool cloth becomes felted wool when it is washed in hot water and dried in a hot dryer. That causes the wool fibers to shrink, pulling them together to make a thick and fuzzy fabric. The design of the fabric—solid, plaid, or stripe—is still visible which gives this cloth a distinct physical and visual texture. Felted wool rarely frays at the edges during stitching.

Wool felt (on the left in the photo above) is made from loose wool fibers that are placed together in layers that run alternately lengthwise and crosswise. The bed of layers is wetted, a little soap is added, and the fibers are rubbed together. The more the fibers are agitated, the tighter the felt will be. Wool felt is solid in appearance and it does not fray.

## Appliqué Templates for Wool Appliqué

Make templates using self-adhesive laminate (see Hand Appliqué Templates, page 17). Templates are used right side down on the paper side of fusible web or right side up on the right side of the wool. Do not add seam allowances to these templates.

Wool appliqué shapes do not require a seam allowance except where one appliqué shape falls beneath another. In that area, you will add a small seam allowance to the bottom shape.

*tip* **X Marks the Spot on Wool Templates** ···

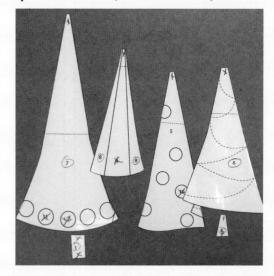

Draw an X on the edge(s) of templates that lie under another shape. You will need to add a small seam allowance in these areas and the X will alert you. Draw the same X onto the fusible web.

# Wool Appliqué with Fusible Web

*There are a few light bulbs in the border blocks that extend over the block seamline and will need to be appliquéd after the blocks are sewn together.*

Fusible web adds stability to the felted wool appliqué pieces. They are less "wiggly" than wool shapes that are only pinned to the block. Should the fusible web come loose as you stitch, place pins in a few key spots to hold the appliqué in place.

SoftFuse Premium, a paper-backed fusible web, is the best choice for fusing felted wool appliqué pieces. I do not recommend other fusible webs, as they can make the appliqué stiff and hard to needle.

Use one large pressing sheet or two smaller Teflon-coated fiberglass pressing sheets with fusible web, to protect the iron and ironing surface and to diffuse and intensify the heat of the iron. Always follow the manufacturer's fusing instructions. SoftFuse Premium instructions tell you to use an iron set at 270° (the wool/silk setting). *Do not use steam.*

## Prepare Wool Appliqué Shapes

**1.** Place each template *right side down* on the paper side of the fusible web. Lightly trace around each template and write the shape's number on the paper.

**2.** Add an additional ⅛″–¼″ seam allowance on those edges that lie below another appliqué shape on the fusible web or by eye when you cut out the shapes. The X on the template (see Tip: X Marks the Spot on Wool Templates, page 29) will help you remember where to add the extra seam allowance.

**3.** Continue tracing shapes on the paper side of the fusible web, leaving ¼″ between shapes.

**4.** Cut out the fusible shapes (both the paper and fusible web) leaving a scant ⅛″ border of paper around each shape.

**5.** Place a nonstick pressing sheet on your ironing surface. Place the wool appliqué fabric right side down on the pressing sheet. Place the appropriate fusible shape on the wrong side of the appliqué fabric with the paper side up.

**6.** Fold the nonstick pressing sheet (or place the second sheet) over the paper and wool. Follow the manufacturer's instructions and use a medium-hot iron to press the fusible web to the wrong side of the appliqué fabric—3–5 seconds is enough. Do not use steam. Do not overpress.

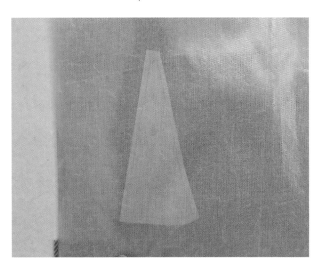

Let the fabric cool and check an edge to be sure the web is fused to the wool. If not, try again.

**7.** Use sharp scissors to cut out the appliqué pieces just inside the drawn line on the paper backing. Leave the paper backing on the appliqué pieces to protect the fusible web until you are ready to fuse them to the background.

## Position and Fuse Wool Appliqué Shapes

**1.** Place a nonstick pressing sheet on your ironing surface. Place the background block flat on it.

**2.** Peel the paper backing off the appliqué shape. Use the placement overlay to position it on the block (see Make a Placement Overlay, page 17).

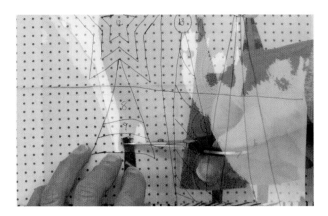

**3.** Look at any seam allowance where one shape lies under another while it is in place, under the placement overlay. If it seems too big, now is the time to trim it.

**4.** Fold the nonstick pressing sheet (or place the second sheet) over the block. Press the wool appliqué shape to the background fabric with a medium-hot iron. The heat must penetrate the thick felted wool, so extend the pressing time to 8–10 seconds. *Do not use steam.*

**5.** Flip the block over, cover it with the pressing sheet, and press it for another 3–5 seconds.

**6.** Let the fabric cool and check an edge to be sure the shape is fused to the background.

# Wool Appliqué with Glue or Pins

When fusible web is not an option, try using a fabric glue stick.

**1.** Place the wool fabric right side up on a sandpaper board.

**2.** Place the template *right side up* on the wool and trace around the shape, using whichever pencil marks the best on your fuzzy wool. Be sure to draw the seam allowance bigger in those places marked with an X (see Prepare Wool Appliqué Shapes, page 30).

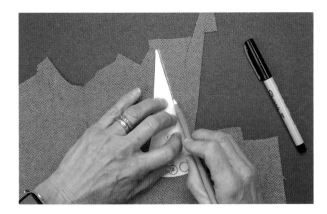

**3.** Cut out the shape, keeping your scissors just inside the drawn line.

**4.** If you are using a glue stick, turn the wool appliqué shape wrong side up on a sandpaper board. Gently cover the back of the shape with glue without stretching or fraying the edges of the shape. Move on to the next step before the glue dries.

**5.** Place your block background right side up the sandpaper board. Place the placement overlay over the block and position the appliqué shape on the background.

**6.** If you are pinning your shapes, pin them to the block (see Pin the Appliqué in Place, page 20).

If you are gluing, once the shape is in position, press it down onto the background. Give the glue a few minutes to dry before you begin stitching.

**7.** If your appliqué comes loose as you stitch, you can reapply glue or place pins in a few key spots to hold the appliqué in place.

# The Whipstitch

The whipstitch is like the invisible appliqué stitch, but bigger. Made with thread in a matching color, the whipstitch holds shapes in place without calling attention to itself. It is a good stitch for these blocks.

**1.** To hide the tail of the thread out of sight, turn your block upside down. Catch ⅜″ of the background fabric with your needle, under the appliqué, near where you will make your first stitch. Pull the thread until it is mostly buried between the wool and the background fabric.

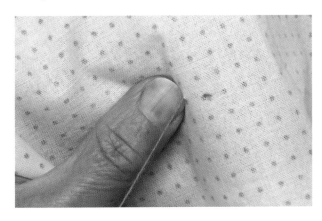

**2.** Make an ending knot on the back of the block, near the edge of the appliqué piece.

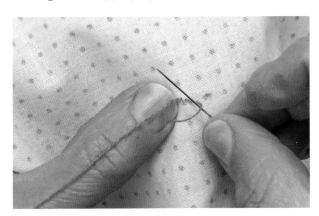

**3.** Hold the block, so the edge to stitch is roughly level with the horizon.

**4.** Bring your thread up from the back of the block, through the appliqué, catching enough of the felted wool, so it will be held in place without fraying the edge. The visible portion of your stitch can range from ¹⁄₁₆″ to ⅛″.

**5.** Position the needle, so it goes straight down into the background fabric, next to the appliqué, and so the stitch you make will be at a 90° angle to the edge.

**6.** Rock the needle over the tip of your middle or index finger underneath the block and push the needle forward, under the background, following the edge of the appliqué.

**7.** Turn the needle point up and push the needle through the background and appliqué, at the same depth as your first stitch. Pull the thread, so it is neither too tight, nor too loose, nestling into the wool and holding the edge in place.

**8.** The position of the hand holding the fabric is important. Place your thumb on top of the edge of the appliqué about a stitch-length away from the beginning of the stitch, so the needle is pointed at the end (not the side) of your thumb as you take a stitch.

As you rock off your bottom fingertip, the thumb holds the layers of fabric together, so your stitch will go straight up through the fabric, rather than on the diagonal.

## Outer Points with the Whipstitch

Three stitches at the outer point form a "chicken foot" to keep your points sharp and stitches pretty.

**1.** When you are 3–4 stitches away from an outer point, begin making slightly smaller stitches. This is especially true for narrow outer points.

**2.** When you reach the point, make a stitch directly over the end of the point. Your needle will enter the background at the end of the point and turn to come up in the appliqué on the second side of the point.

**3.** Resume your normal stitch length when you are past the point.

*tip* **Very Pointy Wool Outer Points** ··········
Sew wool beaks with wool thread in matching colors. If the point is too narrow to stitch through without totally fraying the fabric, take a small stitch or two from side to side, over the point, to hold it in place.

When wool frays at an outer point, take your needle to the back of the block on the first side of the point. Come up through the background at the point.

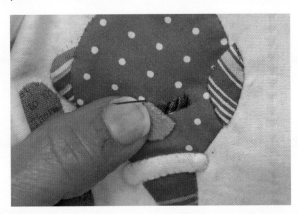

Sew over the point, pushing the needle through the wool point to the back at the base of the chicken foot.

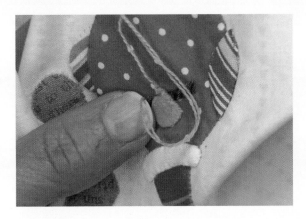

Sew the final stitch of the chicken foot in the same manner, from the edge through the base of the chicken foot to the back.

Bring the needle up just inside the edge of the appliqué to resume your normal stitch.

## Inner Points with the Whipstitch

Just as in invisible appliqué (see Appliqué Inner Points, page 25), there are 3 stitches at an inner point that come together in the background at the deepest part of the inner point. These stitches can be a little deeper than your usual stitch if the wool seems prone to fraying.

**1.** When you reach the inner point, insert the needle into the background fabric next to the edge of the appliqué, at the deepest part of the inner point. Bring the needle up, centered in the appliqué, directly into the inner point.

**2.** Insert the needle once more into the background at the inner point. Turn your needle and come up on the other side of the inner point, mirroring the stitch on the first side of the point.

**3.** Resume your normal stitch once you are past the point.

# Embellishments

## Embroidery

Add embroidery and other soft embellishments to the quilt before it is layered and quilted.

### Stem Stitch

The stem stitch makes very nice bird legs.

**1.** Bring the needle up from underneath the background fabric, at the beginning of the line of stitches at 1.

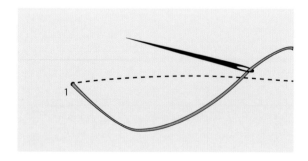

**2.** Move to the right about ¼″ and push the needle through the fabric at 2. Turn the needle, so it comes up midway between 1 and 2, at 3. Hold the thread below the line, making sure the needle is above the stitch. Change the spacing between stitches as desired.

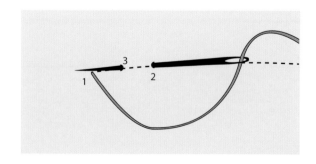

**3.** Pull the needle and thread through the fabric to tighten the stitch, so it lies flat but does not cause the fabric to pucker.

**4.** Move to the right about ¼″ from 3 (⅛″ from 2) and push the needle through the fabric at 4. Turn the needle and come up at 2 in the hole in fabric formed by the last stitch.

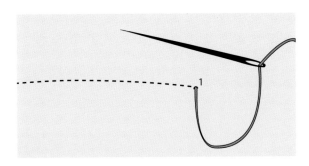

Be sure to hold the thread, so that it drapes over the previous stitch as you make each new stitch.

**5.** Continue in this manner, keeping the stitches uniform in length and tension.

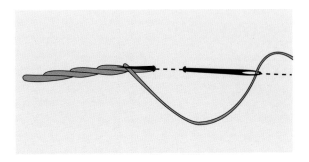

If you turn over the block, the stitches should form a line, from end to end.

## Backstitch

I used the backstitch for the ornament cords.

**1.** Bring the needle up from underneath the background fabric, at the beginning of the line of stitches at 1.

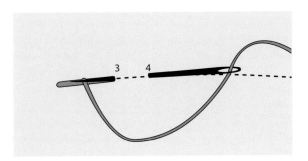

**2.** Move to the left ⅛″ and push the needle through the fabric at 2. Turn the needle, so it comes up ⅛″ away at 3. Change the spacing between stitches as desired.

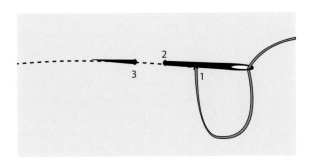

**3.** Pull the needle and thread through the fabric to tighten the stitch, so it lies flat but does not cause the fabric to pucker.

**4.** Insert the needle at 4. Turn the needle and come up ¼″ away at 5. Tighten the stitch, so it lies flat but does not cause the fabric to pucker.

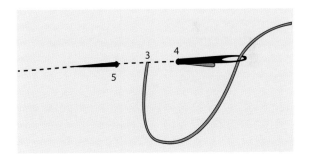

**5.** Continue in this manner, making stitches that are end to end. Adjust the stitch length as desired.

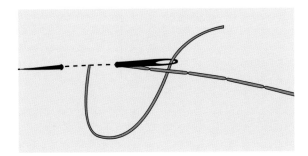

# Couching

Decorative cord and strands of sequins can be sewn in place with thread that is showy or quiet.

**1.** Draw a line on the fabric. The ends of the light cords are hidden in the seams of the blocks. When the ends of the cord are exposed on the block, tuck them under the cord and tack them down with thread. You may have to sew creatively to hide them and that's okay.

**2.** Place the cord over the line and pin or hold it in place.

**3.** Bring the needle up from underneath the background fabric, under the cord at 1, which is marked with a dot in the illustration. Do not catch the cord with the needle. Pull the needle toward you.

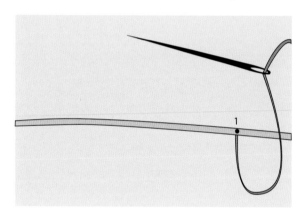

**4.** Insert the needle at 1, on the other side of the cord. Turn the needle, so it comes up at 2. Pull the thread through the fabric to tighten the stitch over the cord.

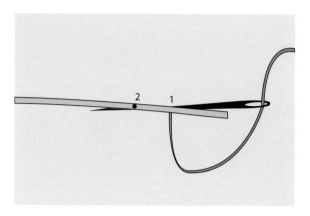

**5.** Continue in this manner, sewing the thicker cord to the block. Adjust the space between stitches as desired.

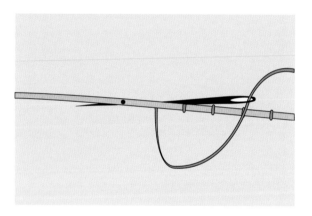

# Ribbon

There are a wide variety of ribbons and trims that are very suitable for *Birds in Toyland* (pages 7 and 8). I used both cotton and silk ribbon, and an invisible stitch and matching thread to sew both sides of these ribbons in place.

Showy thread in the same or contrasting thread can also be used to sew ribbon to your blocks. Use your imagination and have fun embellishing!

## Sequins, Beads, and Hard Embellishments

Sequins and beads add a sparkly, festive attitude to your quilt. Buttons come in all shapes and sizes, and they are cute! Once you start looking, you can find all sorts of creative objects to add to your quilt.

Send the needle and thread through the batting when adding embellishments that are close to each other. Backstitch before traveling to the next spot to secure the stitches. Bury ending knots between the layers of the quilt.

I recommend adding sequins, beads, and other hard embellishments to the quilt after it has been quilted and bound because they can get in the way during quilting.

Sew through all the layers, cinching the embellishments to the quilt using a double strand of thread.

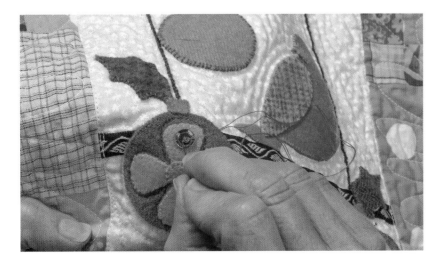

# Appliqué Blocks

You have lots of options for making your blocks. You can appliqué with wool, woven fabrics, or both. You can add lots of embellishments (see Embellishments, page 36)—or let the fabric speak for itself. Have fun with these designs!

Refer to the techniques in the book that correspond to those you use in your own blocks.

There are three photos for each block shown. The first block in each grouping is from my wool quilt *Birds in Toyland* (page 7). The second block in each grouping is from my needle-turned cotton quilt *Birds in Toyland II* (page 63). The third block in each grouping is from Linda Jenkins's wool and cotton quilt *Birds in Toyland III* (page 8).

## Block 1

# Block 2

# Block 3

# Block 4

# Block 5

# Block 6

# Block 7

# Block 8

# Block 9

# Block 10

Block 11

# Block 12

Block 13

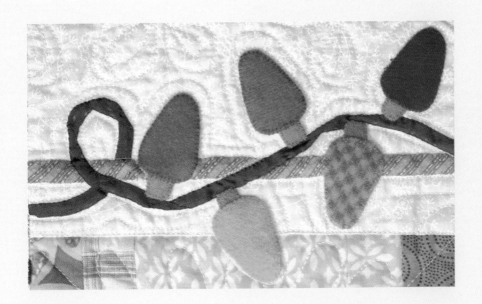

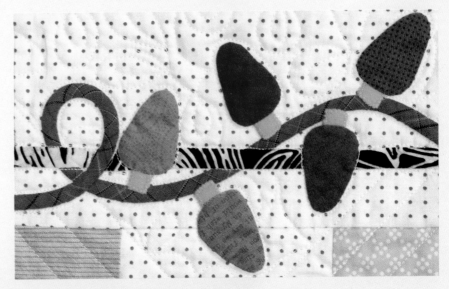

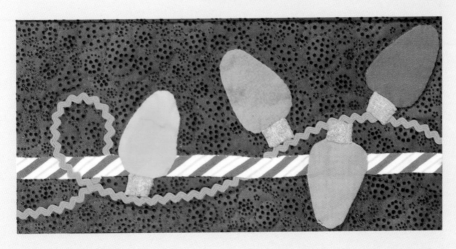

# Border 15

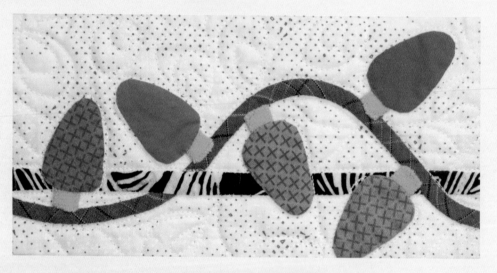

# Border 16

# Border 17

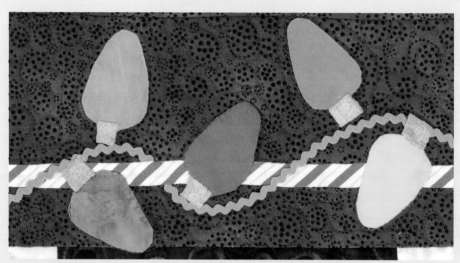

# Border Corner 18

# Quilt Assembly and Finishing

## Press and Trim the Appliqué Blocks and Borders

**1.** Press the appliqué blocks and borders, right side down. Press the wool appliqué and/or embellished blocks on top of a towel to provide a softer surface for pressing.

**2.** Use rotary tools and trim the appliqué blocks to 8½″ × 8½″ (10½″ × 10½″).

**3.** Trim the appliqué border blocks to 4½″ × 8½″ (5½″ × 10½″).

**4.** Trim the appliqué border corner blocks to 4½″ × 4½″ (5½″ × 5½″).

## Set the Quilt Together

**1.** If you have not already done so, make your pieced blocks and borders.

**2.** Place all the blocks and borders in position on your design wall. Take a photograph of your quilt for reference, because it is easy to flip blocks as you handle them.

**3.** Sew the blocks together in rows. Press the seam allowances toward the appliqué blocks.

**4.** Sew the rows together. Press the seam allowances in the direction they lie flattest.

**5.** Complete the appliqué in the borders where the light bulbs lie over adjacent blocks.

## Layer, Baste, and Quilt

Once the quilting is complete, use rotary tools to trim away the excess batting and backing from the outer edges of the quilt, leaving ¼″ of backing and batting extending beyond the edge of the quilt top. This extra fabric and batting will fill the binding nicely.

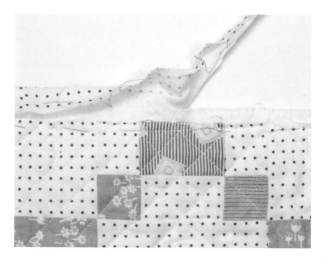

## Add Binding

Binding cut on the straight of grain is less stretchy than bias binding, which is suitable for a wall quilt. The 2½″-wide cut size of the binding strips are for approximately ¼″-finished double-fold binding. Use your favorite method to attach the binding.

## Add a Hanging Sleeve

Placing a hanging sleeve on your quilt ensures it will never be nailed to the wall.

**1.** Cut or construct a strip 8½″ × the width of your quilt.

**2.** Hem the short ends of the strip with matching thread.

**3.** Fold the strip in half wrong sides together, lengthwise. Match the raw edges and sew the sleeve strip into a tube.

**4.** Place the sleeve on your ironing board with the seam centered. Press the seam allowance open and the sleeve flat.

**5.** Turn the sleeve over to be right side up on your ironing board and press an additional lengthwise crease ½″ away from the fold at the bottom of the sleeve. This creates a little fullness in the sleeve to accommodate the thickness of the rod.

**6.** Center the top edge of the sleeve on the top, back of your quilt just below the binding. Hide the seam allowance against the quilt back. Pin or baste it in place.

**7.** With the sleeve flat, lift the top layer of the sleeve to expose the third crease. Pin or baste the sleeve in place along this crease.

**8.** Hand sew the sleeve to the back of the quilt after you have added embellishments.

## Document Your Quilt

The future owners of your quilt will want to know about this quilt! Make and attach a documentation patch. It can be computer generated, embroidered, or hand-written with a permanent fabric pen. Add appliqué, photo transfers—whatever seems right to you.

Include your name, location, and the date. Your quilt may need to be washed, so include the fiber content. Share the name of the pattern you used. If you made the quilt for a special person or occasion, be sure to include that as well.

Artists sign the front of their paintings—you can sign the front of your quilt! Appliqué, embroider, or quilt your name or initials and the date on the quilt top.

> *tip* **Hidden Documentation** ................
> You can write or embroider your name and the date directly on the quilt back, under the sleeve. If the documentation patch is removed, your name will remain on the quilt.

**1.** Make a label for your quilt and hem the edges.

**2.** Hand stitch the label to the back of your quilt.

# Gallery

*The Birds' Christmas Party* by Polly Clarke Stephenson

*2020 Christmas* by Dotti Jones

*Christmas Bird House* by Linda Jenkins

*A Pink Partridge Christmas*
by Denise Plonski

*Snowman's Blue Bird Friend* by Linda Jenkins

*Merry Christmas* by Linda Jenkins

*Hanging Blue Bird and Ornaments* by Linda Jenkins

*Winter Birds* by Linda Jenkins

*Birds in Toyland II* by Becky Goldsmith

To download the project instructions, see Option 2: Downloading the Blocks (page 11).

*Balancing Birds* by Linda Jenkins

To download the project instructions, see Option 2: Downloading the Blocks (page 11).

*Birds in Toyland* by Judy Adock

*Happy Birds in Toyland* by Kathy Rathbun

*Silly Birds in Toyland* by Teri Weed

*Birds in Toyland* by Sharon Noble

# Bonus Downloadable Projects

### Bonus Downloadable Project— Alternate Setting: BIRDS IN TOYLAND II

I simplified the pieced setting and border blocks in this quilt. Look closely and you will see that the corners in these blocks are not pieced four-patches—they are full squares. That changed the yardage, cutting, and piecing instructions a little bit.

To download the project instructions, see Option 2: Downloading the Blocks (page 11).

### Bonus Downloadable Project— BALANCING BIRDS

Spread holiday cheer with this cute quilt that says "Merry Christmas" in a most festive way!

To download the project instructions, see Option 2: Downloading the Blocks (page 11).

# Appliqué Patterns

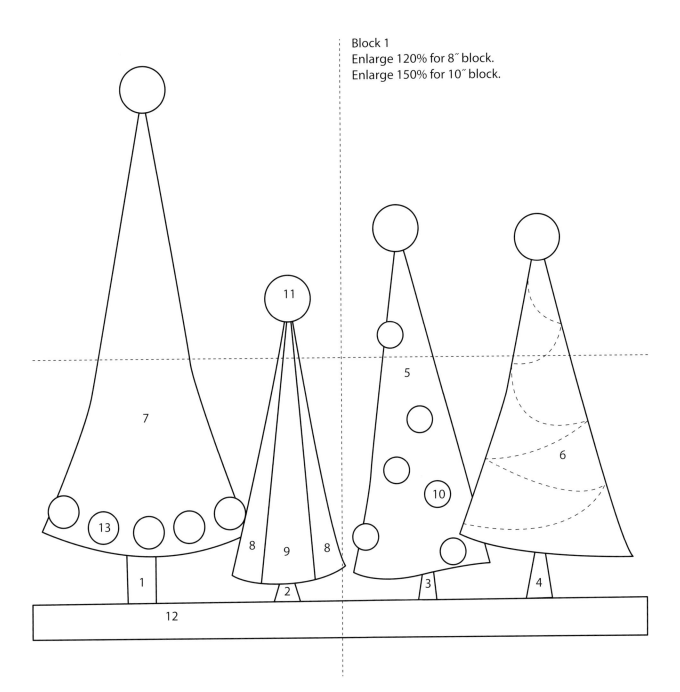

Block 1
Enlarge 120% for 8″ block.
Enlarge 150% for 10″ block.

7

11

5

6

10

13

8    9    8

1

2

3

4

12

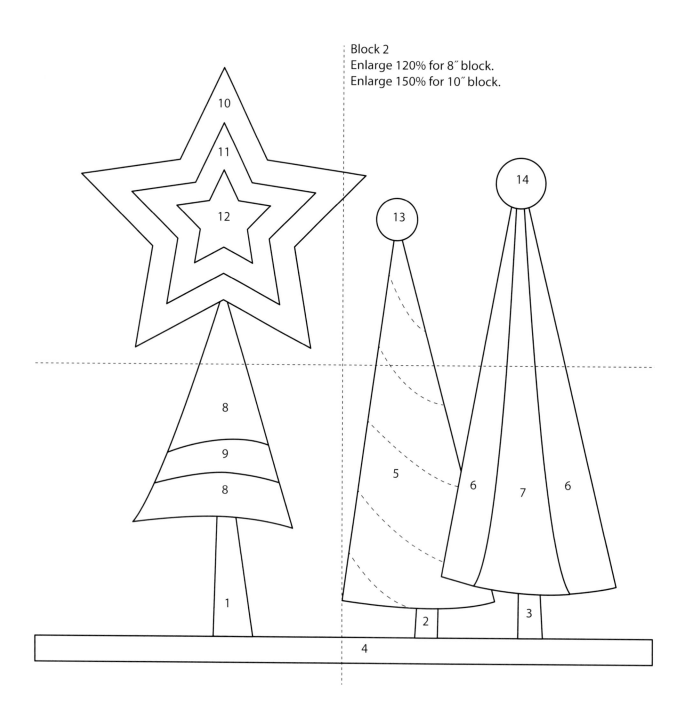

Block 2
Enlarge 120% for 8″ block.
Enlarge 150% for 10″ block.

10

11

12

13

14

8

9

8

5

6

7

6

1

2

3

4

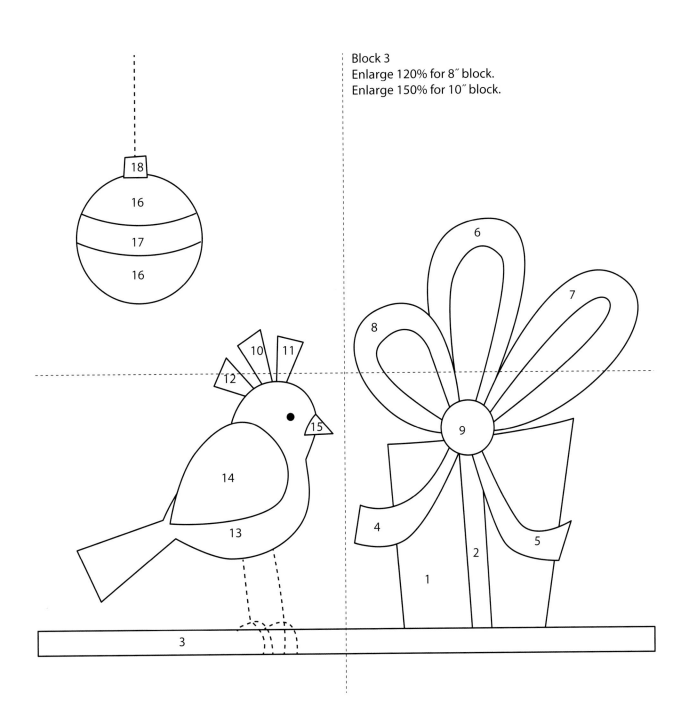

Block 3
Enlarge 120% for 8″ block.
Enlarge 150% for 10″ block.

18

16

17

16

6

7

8

10   11

12

15

9

14

4

13

5

2

1

3

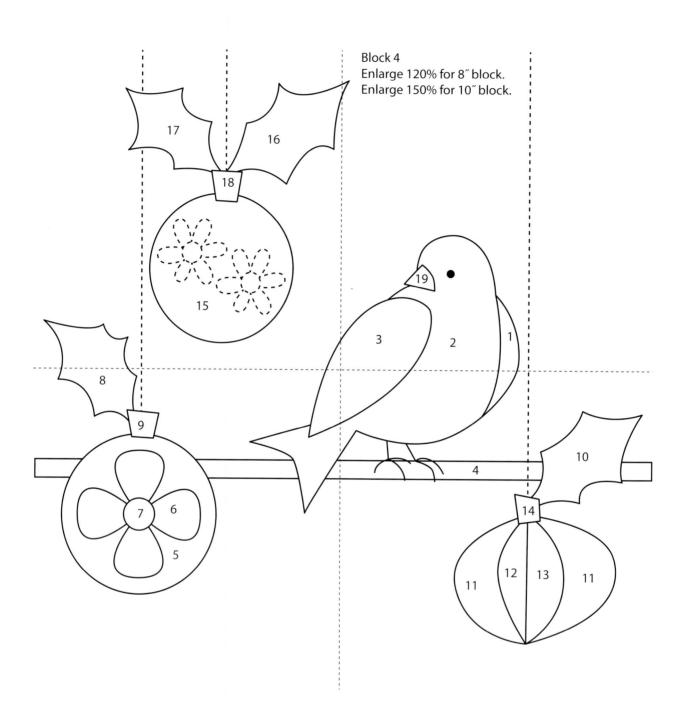

Block 4
Enlarge 120% for 8″ block.
Enlarge 150% for 10″ block.

17

16

18

15

8

9

19

3

2

1

7

6

5

4

10

14

12

13

11

11

Block 5
Enlarge 120% for 8″ block.
Enlarge 150% for 10″ block.

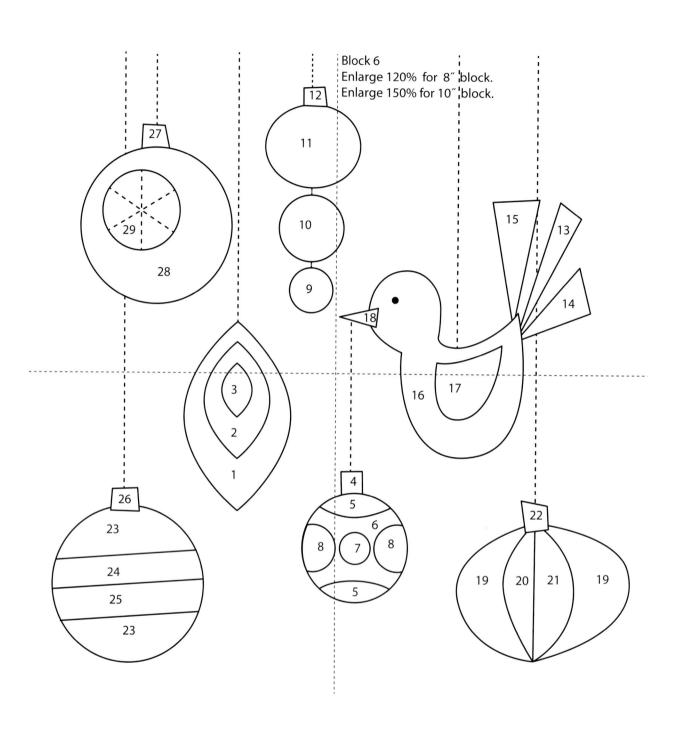

Block 6
Enlarge 120% for 8″ block.
Enlarge 150% for 10″ block.

27

12

11

29
28

10

9

15

13

14

18

16
17

3
2
1

26

23

24

25

23

4
5
6
8   7   8
5

22

19   20   21   19

Block 7
Enlarge 120% for 8″ block.
Enlarge 150% for 10″ block.

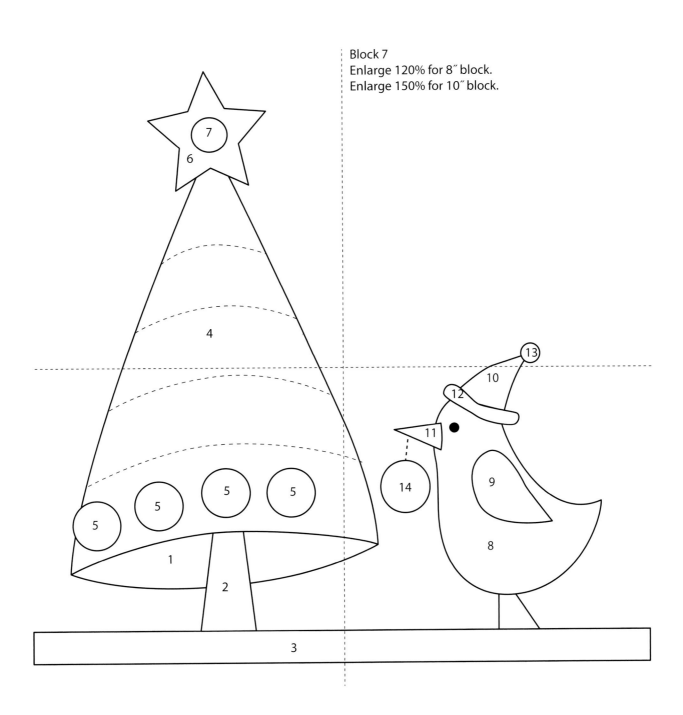

Block 8
Enlarge 120% for 8″ block.
Enlarge 150% for 10″ block.

Block 9
Enlarge 120% for 8″ block.
Enlarge 150% for 10″ block.

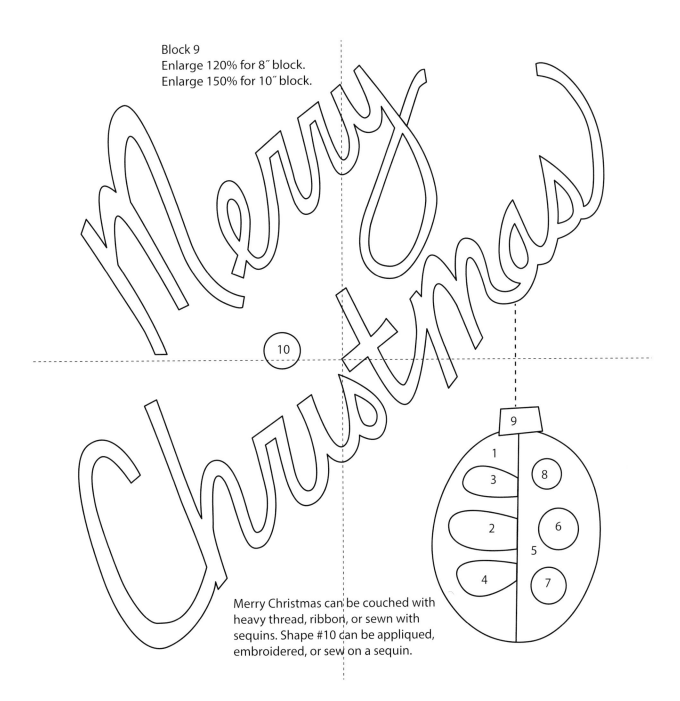

Merry Christmas can be couched with heavy thread, ribbon, or sewn with sequins. Shape #10 can be appliqued, embroidered, or sew on a sequin.

Block 10
Enlarge 120% for 8″ block.
Enlarge 150% for 10″ block.

Block 11
Enlarge 120% for 8˝ block.
Enlarge 150% for 10˝ block.

Block 12
Enlarge 120% for 8″ block.
Enlarge 150% for 10″ block.

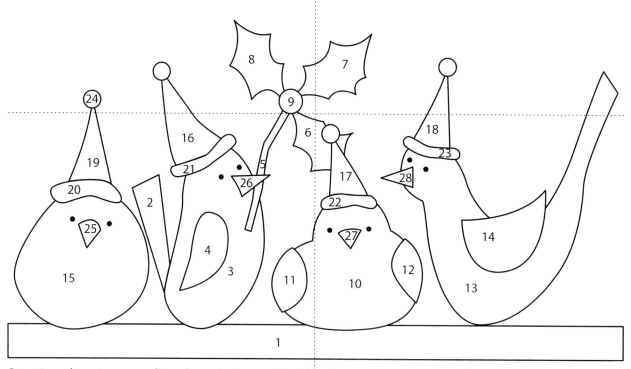

Stem 5 can be cutaway appliqued, couched, or embroidered.

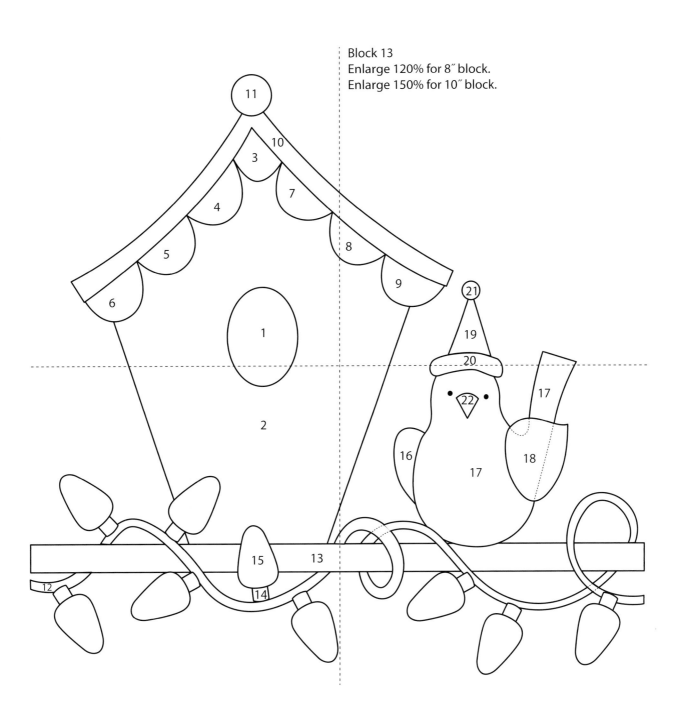

Block 13
Enlarge 120% for 8″ block.
Enlarge 150% for 10″ block.

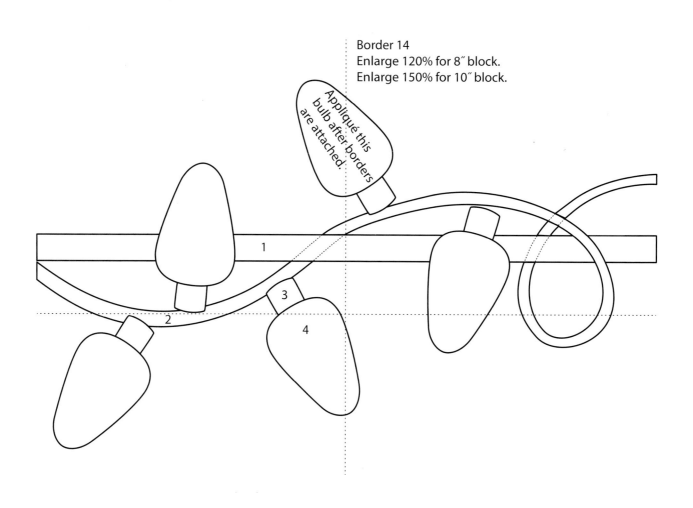

Border 14
Enlarge 120% for 8″ block.
Enlarge 150% for 10″ block.

Appliqué this bulb after borders are attached.

1

2

3

4

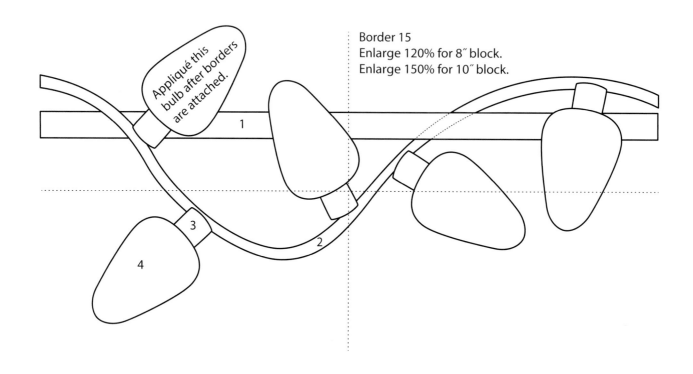

Border 15
Enlarge 120% for 8″ block.
Enlarge 150% for 10″ block.

Appliqué this bulb after borders are attached.

1

2

3

4